Copyright © 1983 Lion Publishing

Published by
Lion Publishing
Icknield Way, Tring, Herts, England
ISBN 0 85648 455 5
Albatross Books
PO Box 320, Sutherland, NSW 2232, Australia
ISBN 0 86760 312 7

Compiled by Ruth Connell

First edition 1983

Matthew 6:9–13 quoted from The Holy Bible,
New International Version: copyright © New York
International Bible Society, 1978

Other Bible quotations from:
Revised Standard Version, copyright 1946 and
1952, second edition 1971, Division of Christian
Education, National Council of the Churches of
Christ in the USA

Printed in Great Britain by
Purnell and Sons (Book Production) Ltd,
Paulton, Bristol

Famous Bible Passages

OUR
FATHER

Matthew 6

A LION BOOK

Our Father in heaven,
hallowed be your name,
your kingdom come,
your will be done
on earth as it is in heaven.
Give us today our daily bread.
Forgive us our debts,
as we also have forgiven our debtors.
And lead us not into temptation,
but deliver us from the evil one.
For yours is the kingdom
And the power
And the glory
For ever.
Amen.

Matthew 6:9–13

OUR Father

When we pray, we pray not for one, but for the whole people, because we the whole people are one.

Cyprian

We must pray, not only alone and for ourselves, but with and for others; for we are members one of another, and we are called into fellowship with each other.

Matthew Henry

His tongue may be unintelligible to me, his customs strange, the pigment of his skin different, but if, through the faith of the Lord Jesus, he has been taught of the Holy Spirit to look up to God and say, 'Father,' I bind him to my heart in a bond dearer than any earthly tie.

J.C. Macaulay

There should be no situation in our life, no attitude, no preoccupation or relationship, from which we cannot look up to this God of absolute Truth and say 'Our Father' of ourselves and of all other souls involved.

Evelyn Underhill

Our FATHER

*What would he not now give to sons when they ask, when he
has already given them this very position of sonship?*
Augustine

*The clear and fixed contemplation of God is the beginning of
all true prayer, and that contemplation does not fasten on his
remote and partially intelligible attributes, nor strive to climb
to behold him as in himself, but grasps him as related to us.*
Alexander MacLaren

*When we approach God, our Father, we are drawing close to
him who completely understands us.*
Phillip Keller

*God is yearning for people who behave like children towards
him and are dependent upon him. As a Father, God would
like to intervene and care for his children.*
Basilea Schlink

*How great care touches the mind of one who says, 'Our
Father' that he be not unworthy of so great a Father.*
Ivo of Chartres

In heaven

As our Father 'in heaven' he is lifted clear above earth's limitations, changes, and imperfections. So child-like familiarity is sublimed into reverence, our hearts are drawn upward, and delivered from the oppressive and narrowing attachment to earth and sense.

Alexander MacLaren

Heaven is what it is by virtue of the fact that his presence, power, conduct, and character make it such.

Phillip Keller

This is what the Lord says:
'Heaven is my throne
and the earth is my footstool.'

Isaiah 66:1

The thought is not that he is only in heaven, yet heaven is his glorious abode . . . This prayer is intended for the disciples on earth who raise their hearts and their eyes to heaven, their future home. Our guarantee for this hope is the fact that our Father is in heaven.

R.C.H. Lenski

Hallowed be your name

God's name, God's kingdom, God's will must be the primary object of Christian prayer. Of course it is not as if God needed our prayers, but they are the means by which the disciples become partakers in the heavenly treasure for which they pray. Furthermore, God uses their prayers to hasten the coming of the end.

Dietrich Bonhoeffer

When we come into our Father's presence, our Lord seems to say, we should be so filled with the thought of him that we forget all about ourselves, our hopes, our needs, even our sins; what we want most of all and therefore utter first is that all men may know how glorious God is and reverence him accordingly — 'Hallowed be Thy Name.'

William Temple

A man can glorify God in no other way save by his virtue which bears witness that the Divine Power is the cause of his goodness.

Gregory of Nyssa

Our response to each experience which he puts in our path, from the greatest disclosure of beauty to the smallest appeal to love, from perfect happiness to utmost grief, will either hallow or not hallow his name.

Evelyn Underhill

The Father's name will not be hallowed throughout the world unless his royal rule be acknowledged.

William Hendriksen

Holiness always dwells, and permanently remains, in God: but men obscure it by their malice and depravity, or dishonour and pollute it by sacrilegious contempt.

John Calvin

Heaven is not the place to glorify God; it will be the place to praise him. The place to glorify him is here.

Watchman Nee

Your kingdom come

Once, having been asked by the Pharisees when the kingdom of God would come, Jesus replied, 'The kingdom of God does not come visibly, nor will people say, "Here it is," or "There it is," because the kingdom of God is within you.'

Luke 17:20–21

It is not our words and our gestures . . . that give glory to the name of God, it is our being the kingdom, which is the radiance and the glory of our maker and our saviour.

Anthony Bloom

The completion of our repentance and the coming of the kingdom are not cause and effect; they are the same thing viewed from different sides.

William Temple

Learn indifference to all that lies outside you and devote yourself to the life within, and you will see the kingdom of God coming in you. The kingdom of God means finding our peace and our joy in the Holy Spirit, and the worldly cannot receive it.

Thomas à Kempis

The knowledge of God is the deepest want of men, and the spread of that knowledge and reverence the way by which his kingdom comes.

Alexander MacLaren

As the blind do not have this present light, so the kingdom of God, although it is everywhere, nevertheless is lacking for those who do not know.

Ivo of Chartres

The present quality of life among the people of God is to be a sign of that coming perfection and justice which will be revealed when the kingdoms of this world finally and completely become the kingdom of our Lord.

Ronald Sider

Father, you long to rule. But you want the world to choose you. May your love spread everywhere. May more and more men and women make you King of their lives.

Andrew Knowles

Your will be done

We who wish to abide for ever ought to do the will of God who is for ever.

Cyprian

The wise man knows that nothing is more important than to discover the general will of God for all his people in Scripture; and to discover the particular will of God for each individual, partly from Scripture, partly in prayer, partly through discussing the issue with others, and partly through using the minds that God has given us.

John Stott

In fellowship with Jesus his followers have surrendered their own wills completely to God's, and so they pray that God's will may be done throughout the world. No creature on earth shall defy him. But the evil will is still alive even in the followers of Christ, it still seeks to cut them off from fellowship with him; and that is why they must also pray that the will of God may prevail more and more in their hearts every day and break down all defiance. In the end the whole world must bow before that will, worshipping and giving thanks in joy and tribulation.

Dietrich Bonhoeffer

'Thy will be done', not as an alien will, not as a will strong and able to break us, but as a will with which we have become completely harmonious.

Anthony Bloom

The petition . . . is not that I may patiently suffer God's will but also that I may vigorously do it. I must be an agent as well as a patient. I am asking that I may be enabled to do it.
C.S. Lewis

Let a man sanctify the Lord God in his heart and he can therefore do no common act. All he does is good and acceptable to God through Jesus Christ. For such a man, living itself will be sacramental and the whole world a sanctuary.
A.W. Tozer

We come closest to God not when, with our mind, we obtain a wide conspectus of truth, but when in our purposes we are united with his righteous purpose.
William Temple

Not that any one can hinder the doing of God's will, but we ask that his will may be done by all men.
Tertullian

We pray that neither our will nor any other man's will, but his will alone may be done, and that what he plans and counsels may succeed and overcome all the schemes and undertakings of the world, as well as everything else that may set itself against his plans and counsels, even though the whole world were to mass itself and rally all its strength to defend its cause against him.
Martin Luther

True holiness consists in doing God's will with a smile.
Mother Teresa

On earth as it is in heaven

'Thy will be done' is not a submissive readiness to bear God's will, as we often take it to be. It is the positive attitude of those who . . . set out to make the will of God present and real on earth as it is in heaven.

Anthony Bloom

Thy will be done on earth as it is in heaven; so that we may love thee with all our heart, thinking ever of thee; with all our mind, directing all our intentions to thee, and seeking thy honour in all things; and with all our strength, employing all the power of our spirit and all the senses of our body in the service of thy love, and in naught else: and that we may also love our neighbours as ourselves, drawing all men, as far as it is in our power, toward thy love, rejoicing in the good things of others and grieving at their ills as at our own, and never giving offence to anyone.

Francis of Assisi

We pray that earth may be made more like heaven by the observance of God's will.

Matthew Henry

Give us today our daily bread

Every good and perfect gift is from above, coming down from the Father of the heavenly lights, who does not change like shifting shadows.

James 1:17

The disciple must receive his portion from God every day. If he stores it up as a permanent possession, he spoils not only the gift, but himself as well, for he sets his heart on his accumulated wealth, and makes it a barrier between himself and God. Where our treasure is, there is our trust, our security, our consolation and our God. Hoarding is idolatry.

Dietrich Bonhoeffer

Give me neither poverty nor riches,
but give me only my daily bread.
Otherwise, I may have too much and disown you
and say, 'Who is the Lord?'
Or I may become poor and steal,
and so dishonour the name of my God.

Proverbs 30:8–9

Unless God feeds us daily, the largest accumulation of the necessaries of life will be of no avail. Though we may have abundance of corn and wine, and every thing else, unless they are watered by the secret blessing of God, they will suddenly vanish, or we will be deprived of the use of them, or they will lose their natural power to support us, so that we shall famish in the midst of plenty.

John Calvin

Do not turn your back on the needy, but share everything with your brother and call nothing your own. For if you have what is eternal in common, how much more should you have what is transient!

The Didache

Do not be anxious about tomorrow, for tomorrow will be anxious for itself.

Matthew 6:34

*F*orgive us our debts

Because he knoweth that our nature is so weak that we cannot but sin daily; therefore he teacheth us daily to repent, and to reconcile ourselves together, and daily to ask God's forgiveness.
William Tyndale

A petition for pardon is itself a full confession, because he who begs for pardon fully admits his guilt.
Tertullian

No child of God sins to that degree as to make himself incapable of forgiveness
John Bunyan

*A*s we also have forgiven our debtors

Forgiveness is not an occasional act; it is a permanent attitude.
Martin Luther King Jnr

Be kind and compassionate to one another, forgiving each other, just as in Christ God forgave you.
Ephesians 4:32

Anyone can love his friends; anyone can love people who are kind to him; the test is 'Love your enemies.' That is forgiveness. Treat your enemies as if they were your friends. That is the great test of whether your heart is in tune with God; for that is what God himself does.
William Temple

To be a Christian means to forgive the inexcusable, because God has forgiven the inexcusable in you. This is hard. It is perhaps not so hard to forgive a single great injury. But to forgive the incessant provocations of daily life — to keep on forgiving the bossy mother-in-law, the bullying husband, the nagging wife, the selfish daughter, the deceitful son — how can we do it? Only, I think, by remembering where we stand, by meaning our words when we say in our prayers each night 'Forgive us our trespasses as we forgive those who trespass against us.' We are offered forgiveness on no other terms. To refuse it is to refuse God's mercy for ourselves. There is no hint of exceptions and God means what he says.
C.S. Lewis

The mercy of God to us in forgiving our sins is not made known to the world by any means more than this: when a man is not hard and extreme, but equal and merciful in his dealing with men.

William Perkins

We must not expect our prayers for forgiveness to be heard if we pray with malice and spite in our hearts towards others. To pray in such a frame of mind is mere formality and hypocrisy ... Our prayers are nothing without charity. We must not expect to be forgiven, if we cannot forgive.

J.C. Ryle

God asks only that we treat other people the same way as we are treated.

Merton Kelsey

*A*nd lead us not into temptation

*Let no temptation fall upon us greater than thine help in us;
but be thou stronger in us than the temptation thou sendest, or
lettest come upon us.*

William Tyndale

*Many and diverse are the temptations which beset the
Christian. Satan attacks him on every side, if haply he might
cause him to fall. Sometimes the attack takes the form of a
false sense of security, and sometimes of ungodly doubt. But the
disciple is conscious of his weakness, and does not expose
himself unnecessarily to temptation in order to test the strength
of his faith. Christians ask God not to put their puny faith to
the test, but to preserve them in the hour of temptation.*

Dietrich Bonhoeffer

*Spare us, where possible, from all crises, whether of temptation
or affliction.*

C.S. Lewis

*When troubles and temptations and evil thoughts attack a
man who is trying to do God's will, they make him realize
how necessary God is to him, since he can do no good without
him.*

Thomas à Kempis

*God is faithful, and he will not let you be tempted beyond
your strength, but with the temptation will also provide the
way of escape, that you may be able to endure it.*

1 Corinthians 10:13

But deliver us from the evil one

Jesus, praying for his disciples, said, 'I do not pray that thou shouldst take them out of the world, but that thou shouldst keep them from the evil one.'

John 17:15

We are constantly seeing, hearing, and feeling the presence of evil. It is about us, and within us, and around us on every side; and we entreat him, who alone can preserve us, to be continually delivering us from its power.

J.C. Ryle

When we have once asked for God's protection against evil and have obtained it, then against everything which the devil and the world can do against us, we stand secure and safe. For what fear is there in this life to the man whose guardian in this life is God?

Cyprian

The devil wants slaves, but God wants free men in harmony of will with him.

Anthony Bloom

For yours is the kingdom

God's majesty and love constitute the basis of our confidence that the prayer will be heard.

William Hendriksen

We end the prayer by recognising that God is king, that we are subjects, and by pledging our obedience and our allegiance to him.

William Barclay

The last phrase of the prayer carries the soul forward to an entire self-oblivion, an upward and outward glance of awestruck worship which is yet entinctured with an utter and childlike trust.

Evelyn Underhill

These three things he has reserved for himself — to govern, to judge and to glory.

Martin Luther

*A*nd the power

The ringing testimony of the Christian faith is that God is able.

Martin Luther King Jnr

Our hearts and our eyes cannot be caught and dismayed by daily events, however closely we follow them. Above them, we seek and find God the Lord, and in reverence look upon his works. We seek and find our Lord Jesus Christ, and firmly believe in his victory and in the glory of his community. We seek and find God the Holy Spirit, who gives his word power over us, greater power than the world can ever gain over us.

Dietrich Bonhoeffer

Those who pray this prayer acknowledge that all power belongs to the Father, not only the power over the entire universe and all it contains, but even the power that resides within all.

William Hendriksen

Quotations from copyright material are as follows:
William Barclay, The Plain Man Looks at the
Lord's Prayer, *Collins 1964; Anthony Bloom,*
Living Prayer, *Darton, Longman and Todd 1966;*
Dietrich Bonhoeffer, The Cost of Discipleship,
SCM Press 1959, quote page 36 The Way to
Freedom, *Collins 1966; William Hendriksen,*
Matthew, *Banner of Truth Trust 1974; Phillip*
Keller, A Layman Looks at the Lord's Prayer,
Moody Press 1976; Merton Kelsey, The Other Side
of Silence, *The Missionary Society of St Paul the*
Apostle 1976, SPCK 1977; Thomas à Kempis,
The Imitation of Christ, *translated by Betty I.*
Knott, Collins Fontana 1963; Martin Luther King
Jnr, Strength to Love, *Hodder and Stoughton*
1964; Andrew Knowles, The Way Out, *Fount*
Paperbacks 1977; R.C.H. Lenski, Interpretation of
St Matthew's Gospel, *Wartburg Press 1943; C.S.*
Lewis, Prayer: Letters to Malcolm, *Geoffrey Bles*
1964; J.C. Macaulay, After This Manner,
Eerdmans 1952; Watchman Nee, Love Not the
World, *Victory Press 1970; Basilea Schlink, from*
Father of Comfort, *Oliphants 1971; Ronald Sider,*
Christ and Violence, *Herald Press 1979, Lion*
Publishing 1980; William Temple, in Daily
Readings from William Temple, *compiled by Hugh*
C. Warner, Hodder and Stoughton 1948; Mother
Teresa, quoted in Something Beautiful for God *by*
Malcolm Muggeridge, Collins 1971; A.W. Tozer,
The Pursuit of God, *Christian Publications 1948,*
Marshall, Morgan and Scott 1961; Evelyn
Underhill, Abba, *Longman, Green and Company*
1940

Photographs by Aerofilms: page 17; Sonia Halliday
Photographs: F.H.C. Birch, pages 12, 38, Sister
Daniel pages 11, 15, 23 and cover, 41; Lion
Publishing: David Alexander, pages 29, 43, Jon
Willcocks, pages 18, 21, 25, 27, 31, 33; RIDA
Photolibrary: D.J. Taylor, page 35; ZEFA, page

And the glory

Holy, holy, holy is the Lord of hosts;
the whole earth is full of his glory.

Isaiah 6:3

'The glory' or honour and praise, belongs only to God. No
one may boast of anything, his wisdom or holiness or ability,
except through him and from him.

Martin Luther

Yours, O Lord, is the greatness and the power
and the glory and the majesty and the splendour,
for everything in heaven and earth is yours.
Yours, O Lord, is the kingdom;
you are exalted as head over all.
Wealth and honour come from you;
you are the ruler of all things.
In your hands are strength and power
to exalt and give strength to all.
Now, our God, we give you thanks,
and praise your glorious name.

1 Chronicles 29:11–13

For ever

Before the mountains were born
or you brought forth the earth and the world,
from everlasting to everlasting you are God.

Psalm 90:2

Time began in him and will end in him. To it he pays no
tribute and from it he suffers no change.

A.W. Tozer

I am Alpha and Omega, the beginning and the ending, saith
the Lord, which is, and which was, and which is to come, the
Almighty.

Revelation 1:8

*A*men

God help us, without doubting, to obtain all these petitions, and suffer us not to doubt that thou hast heard us and wilt hear us in them all; that it is 'Yea,' and not 'Nay,' and not 'Perhaps.' Therefore we say with joy, 'Amen — it is true and certain.' Amen

Martin Luther

Amen!
Praise and glory
and wisdom and thanks and honour
and power and strength
be to our God for ever and ever.
Amen!

Revelation 7 : 1 2

Prayer

Almighty God, unto whom all hearts be open, all desires known, and from whom no secrets are hid; Cleanse the thoughts of our hearts by the inspiration of thy Holy Spirit, that we may perfectly love thee, and worthily magnify thy holy Name; through Christ our Lord. Amen.

The Book of Common Prayer